THE SQUISHY THINGS THAT MAKE ME ME!

ORGANS IN MY BODY

Biology 1st Grade
Children's Biology Books

Baby Professor

EDUCATION KIDS

Speedy Publishing LLC

40 E. Main St. #1156

Newark, DE 19711

www.speedypublishing.com

Copyright 2017

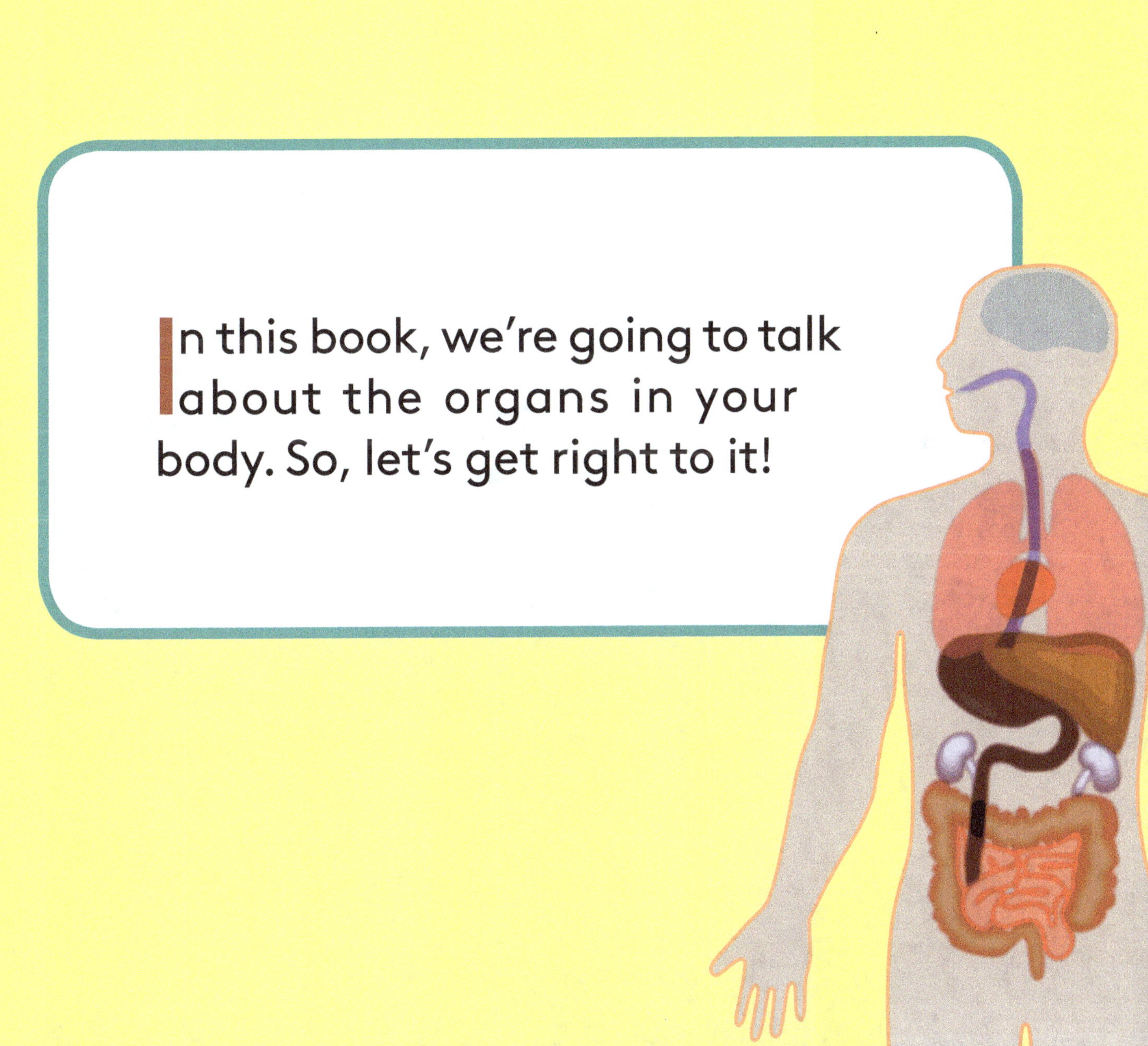

In this book, we're going to talk about the organs in your body. So, let's get right to it!

There are over 70 organs in your body. Organs are groups of cells that are part of all living things. They each have a special job to do. If they do their job well, they keep you healthy.

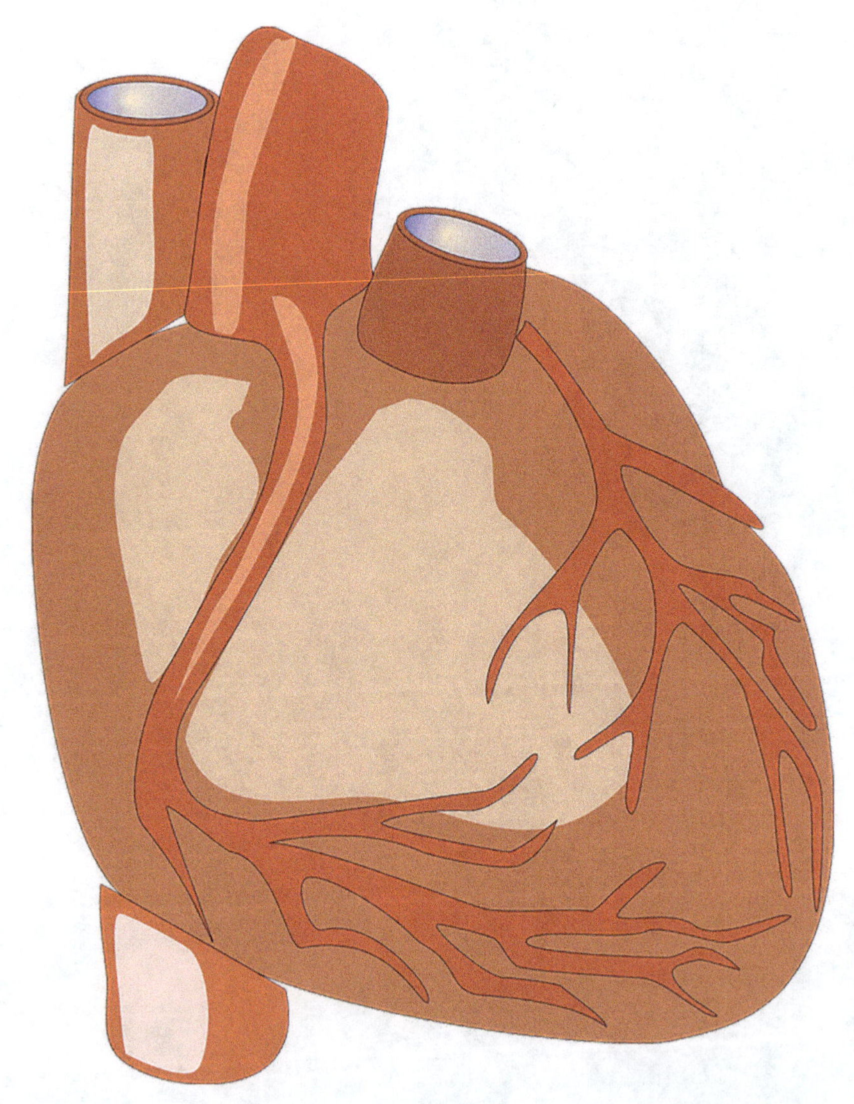

The Human Heart

For the most part, organs are squishy and soft. Certain organs you need to have in order to live. For example, you can't live without a heart, but you can live without a gall bladder. If you ever held a chicken heart in your hands, then you would know what an organ feels like.

THE BRAIN

Your brain is the command center for your body. It's a gray, squishy organ about the size of a cauliflower that has folds in it. You have a hard skull that protects your brain. Your brain works something like a computer does. It takes in the information that you see, hear, and feel and sorts it for you.

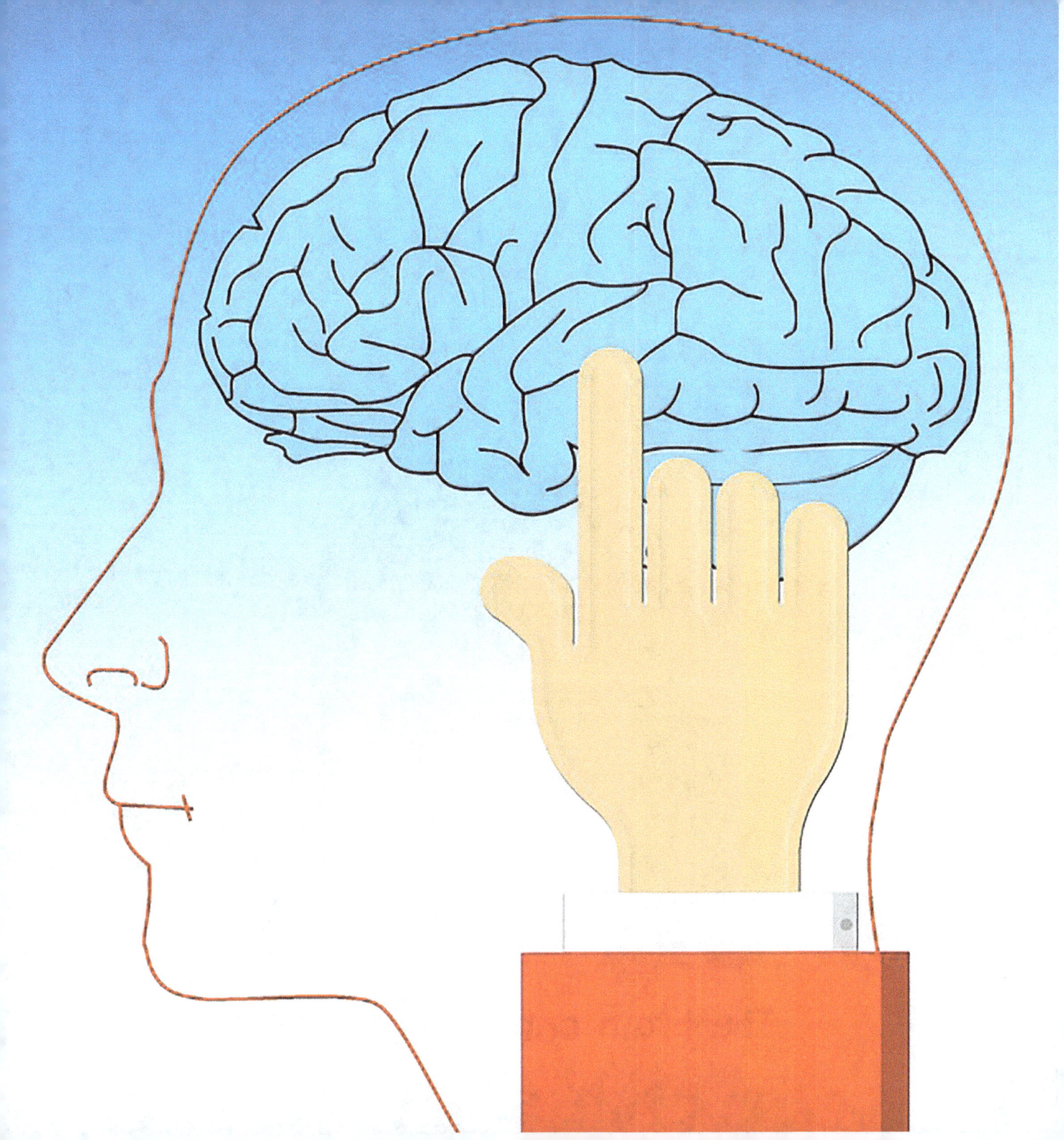

The brain controls our thinking.

Without your brain, the rest of your body couldn't work. Your brain controls your unconscious body processes, which simply means that it controls functions like the beating of your heart. You don't have to think to make your heart beat. It just beats automatically. Your brain also controls the kind of conscious thinking you need to create things, to learn, and to read.

THE HEART

Your heart is about the size of your closed fist and is somewhat cone-shaped. If you touch your chest, you can feel your heart pumping blood throughout your body. Your heart has four chambers.

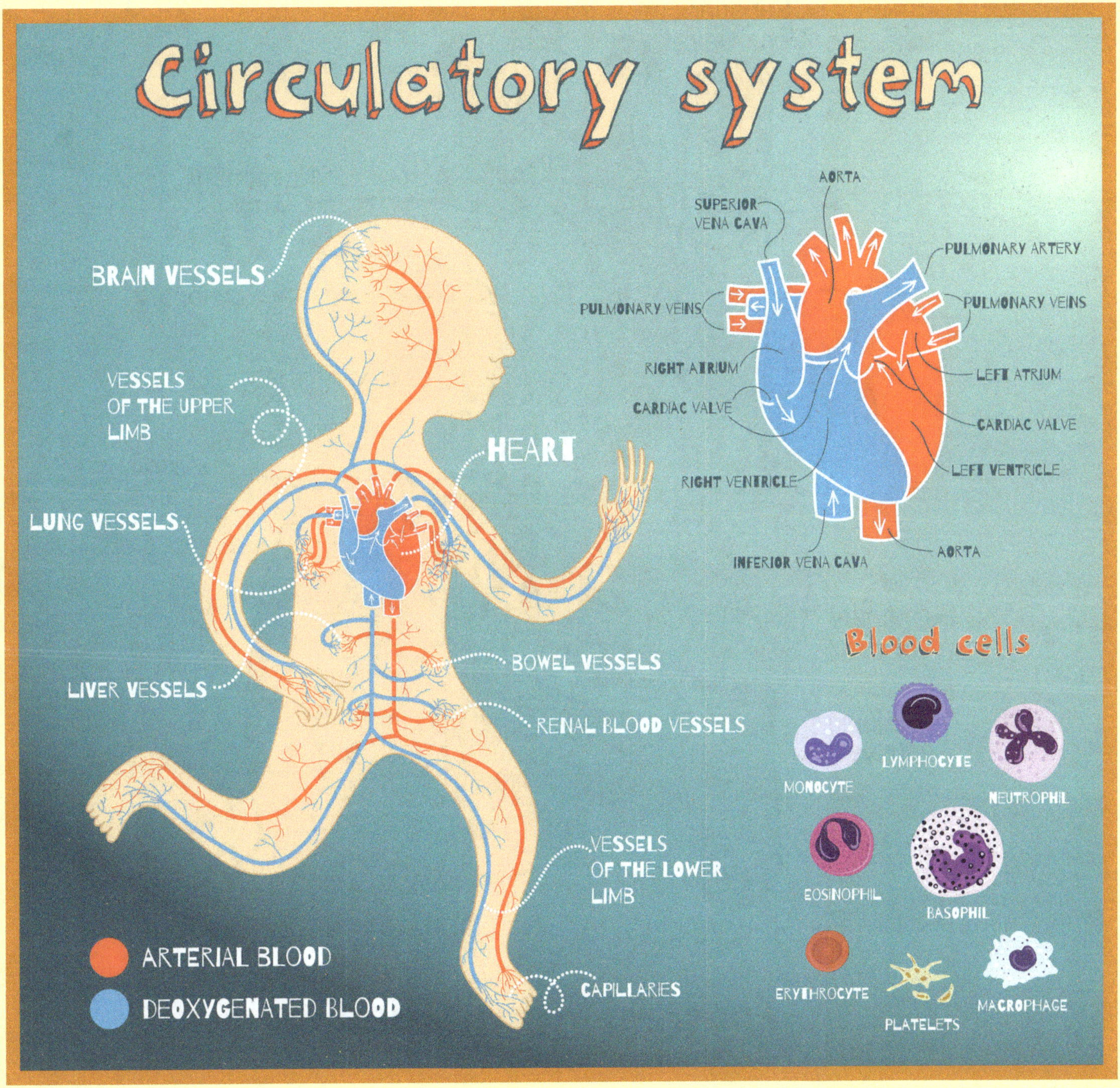

Circulatory system
BRAIN VESSELS
VESSELS OF THE UPPER LIMB
HEART
LUNG VESSELS
LIVER VESSELS
BOWEL VESSELS
RENAL BLOOD VESSELS
VESSELS OF THE LOWER LIMB
CAPILLARIES
ARTERIAL BLOOD
DEOXYGENATED BLOOD
AORTA
SUPERIOR VENA CAVA
PULMONARY VEINS
RIGHT ATRIUM
CARDIAC VALVE
RIGHT VENTRICLE
INFERIOR VENA CAVA
PULMONARY ARTERY
PULMONARY VEINS
LEFT ATRIUM
CARDIAC VALVE
LEFT VENTRICLE
AORTA
Blood cells
MONOCYTE
LYMPHOCYTE
NEUTROPHIL
EOSINOPHIL
BASOPHIL
ERYTHROCYTE
PLATELETS
MACROPHAGE

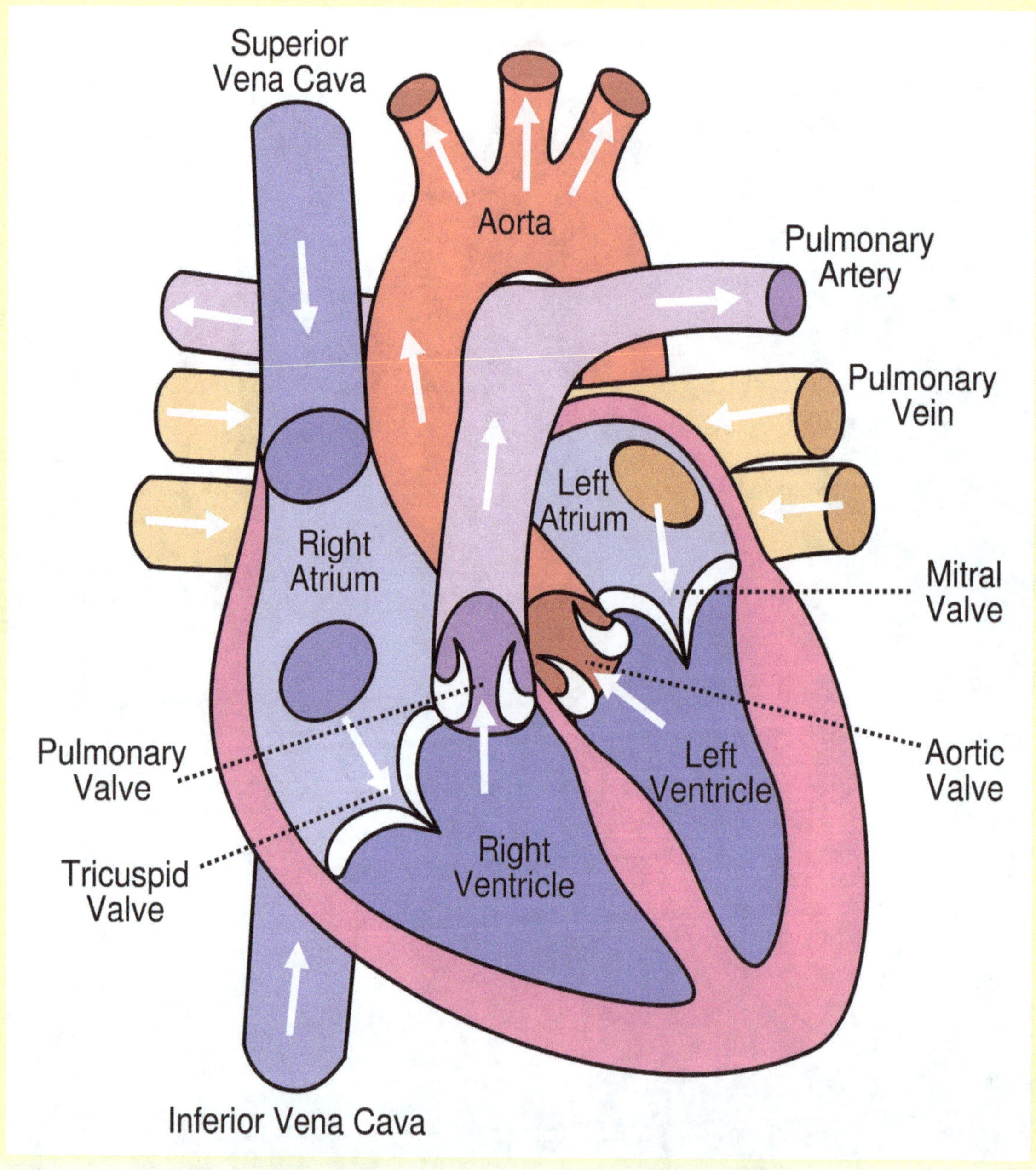

Anatomy of the Heart

The top two chambers of the heart are the atria. The heart's lower chambers are the two ventricles. You can help keep your heart healthy by exercising. Your heart beats about 100,000 times every day. If you live to be 80 years old, your heart will beat 2.5 billion times or more.

Your powerful heart is made of a special type of muscle called cardiac muscle. It works all the time without getting any rest. The valves that keep blood flowing within the chambers in your heart are one-way valves.

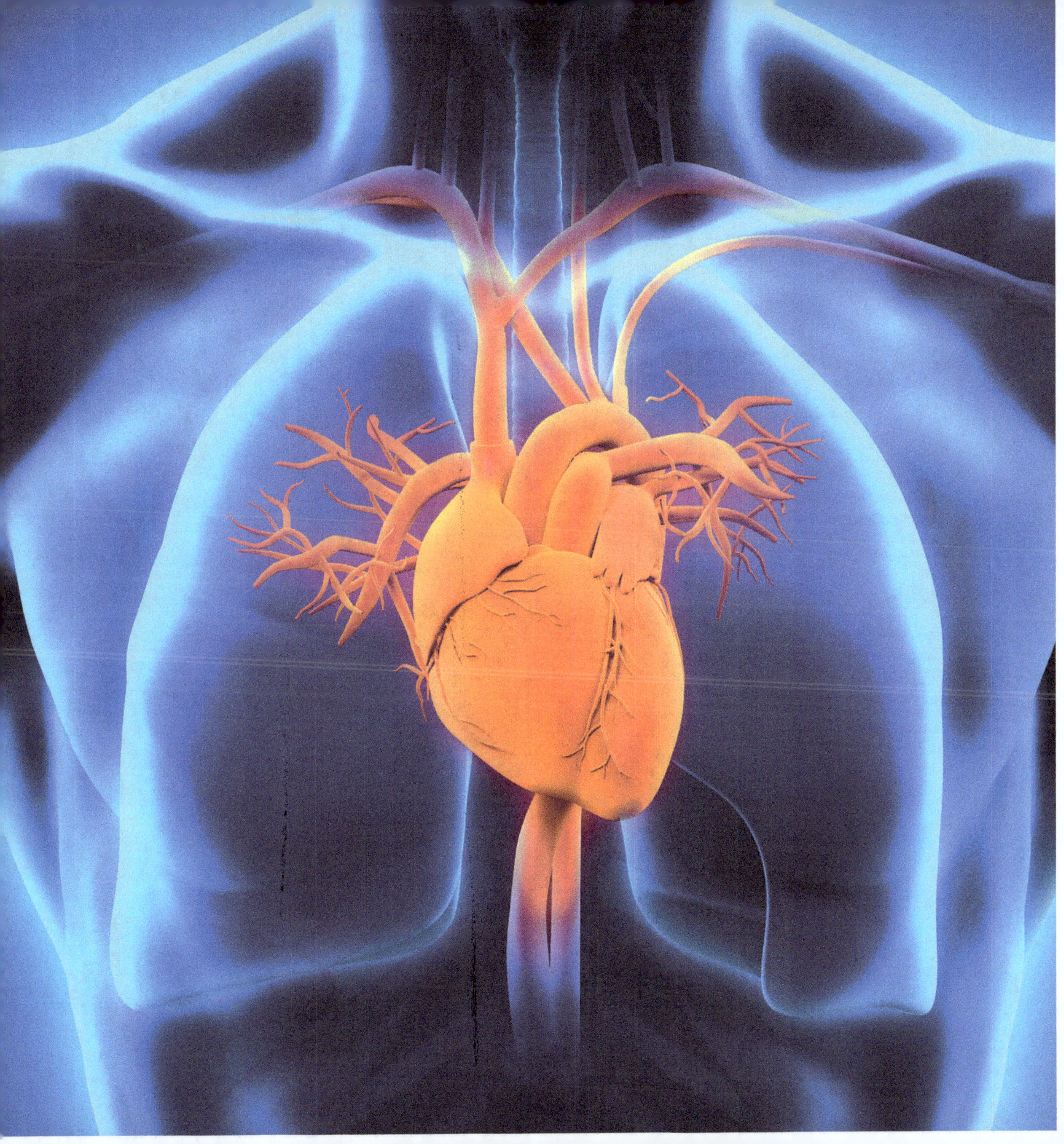

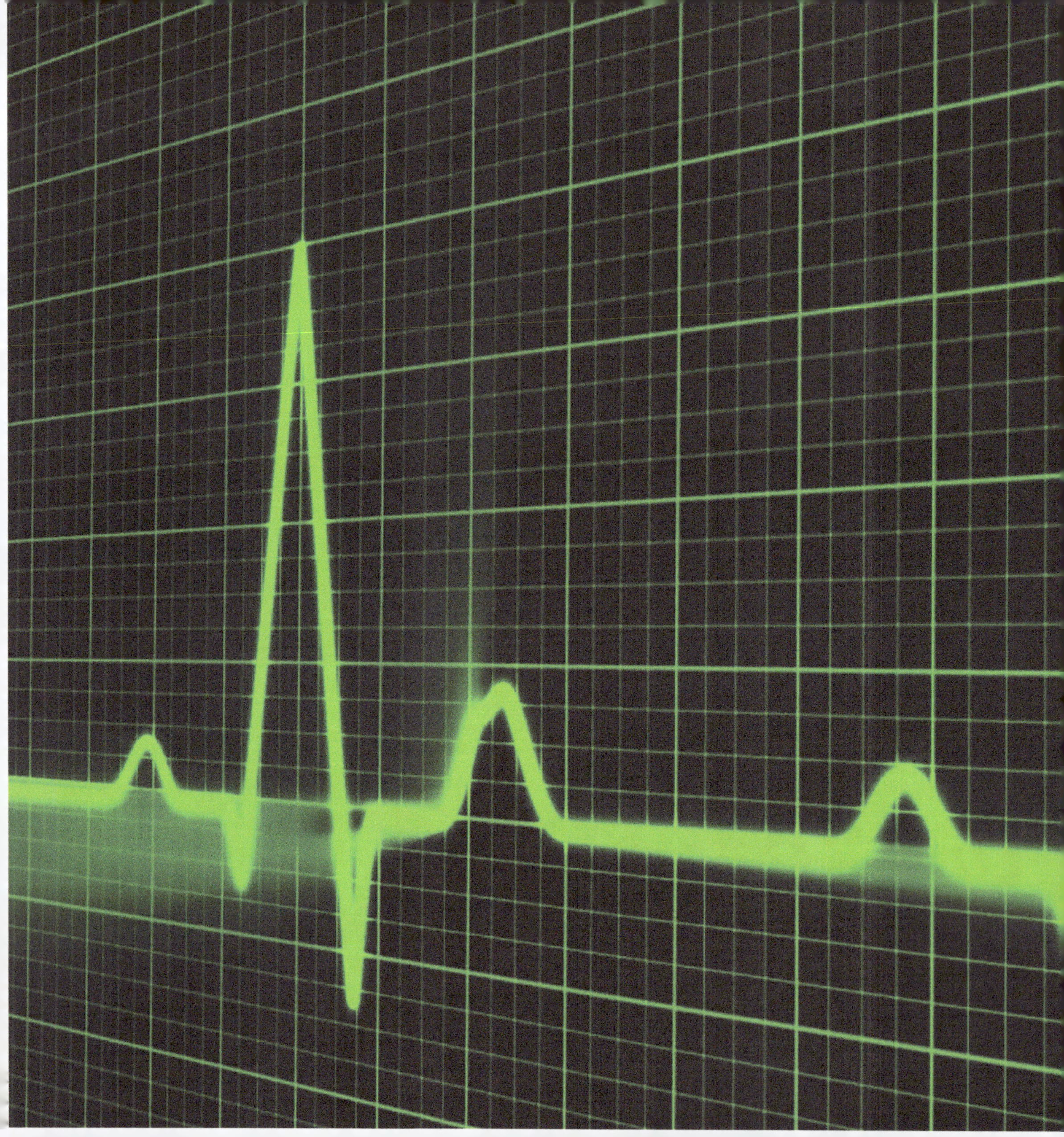

As blood moves from one chamber to a second chamber, the valve it was flowing through closes, so that the blood doesn't flow backwards. As they snap shut, the valves make the thump-thump sound that we know as a heart beat. Your heart is part of the cardiovascular system, which pumps blood throughout your body to all your cells.

THE LUNGS

There are two lungs in your body—a right lung and a left lung. Your right lung is a little larger than your left lung. That's because your heart is on the left side. Your lungs are like large sponges. Using your lungs, you breathe oxygen, which you need to live.

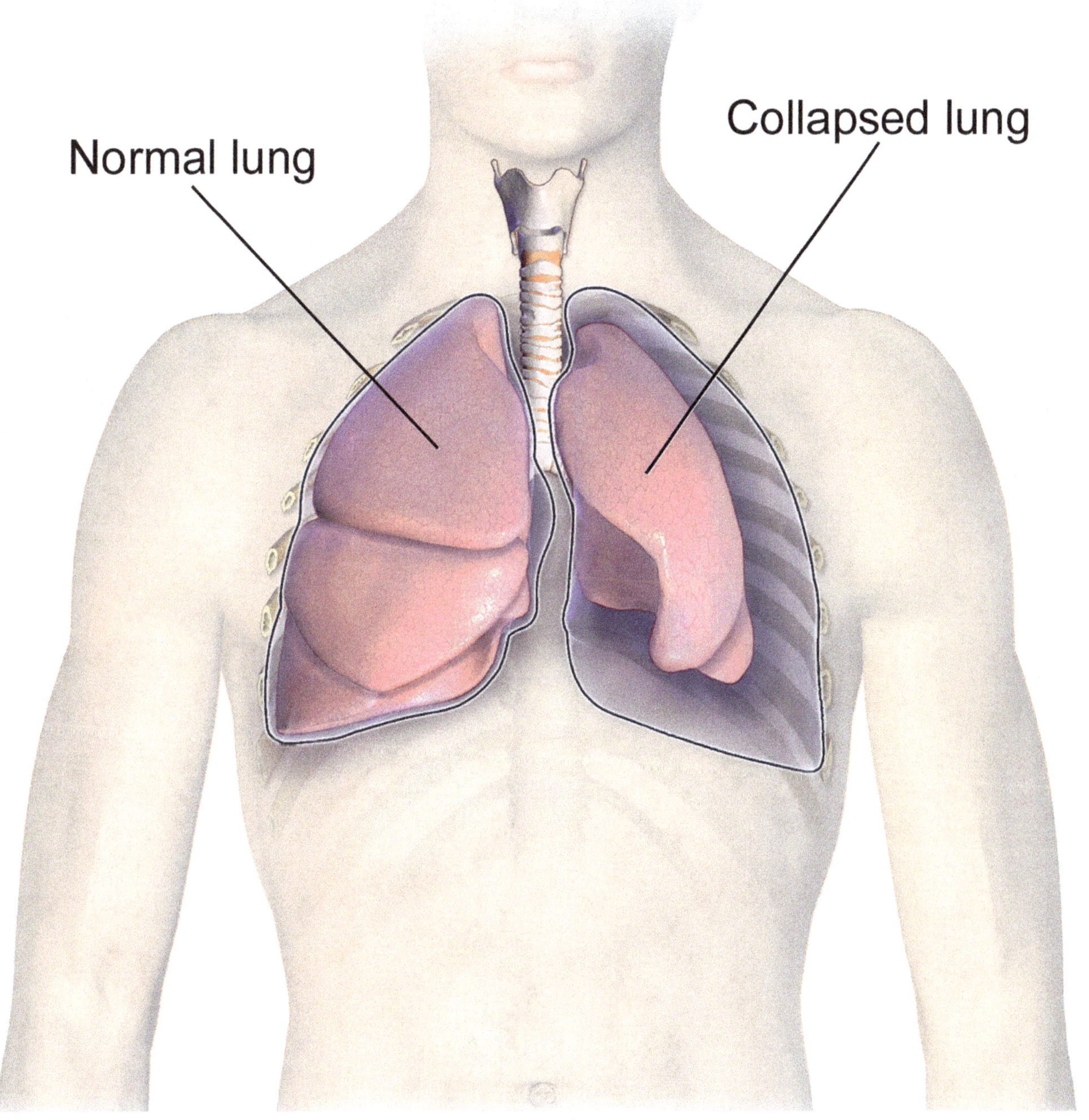

The Human Lungs

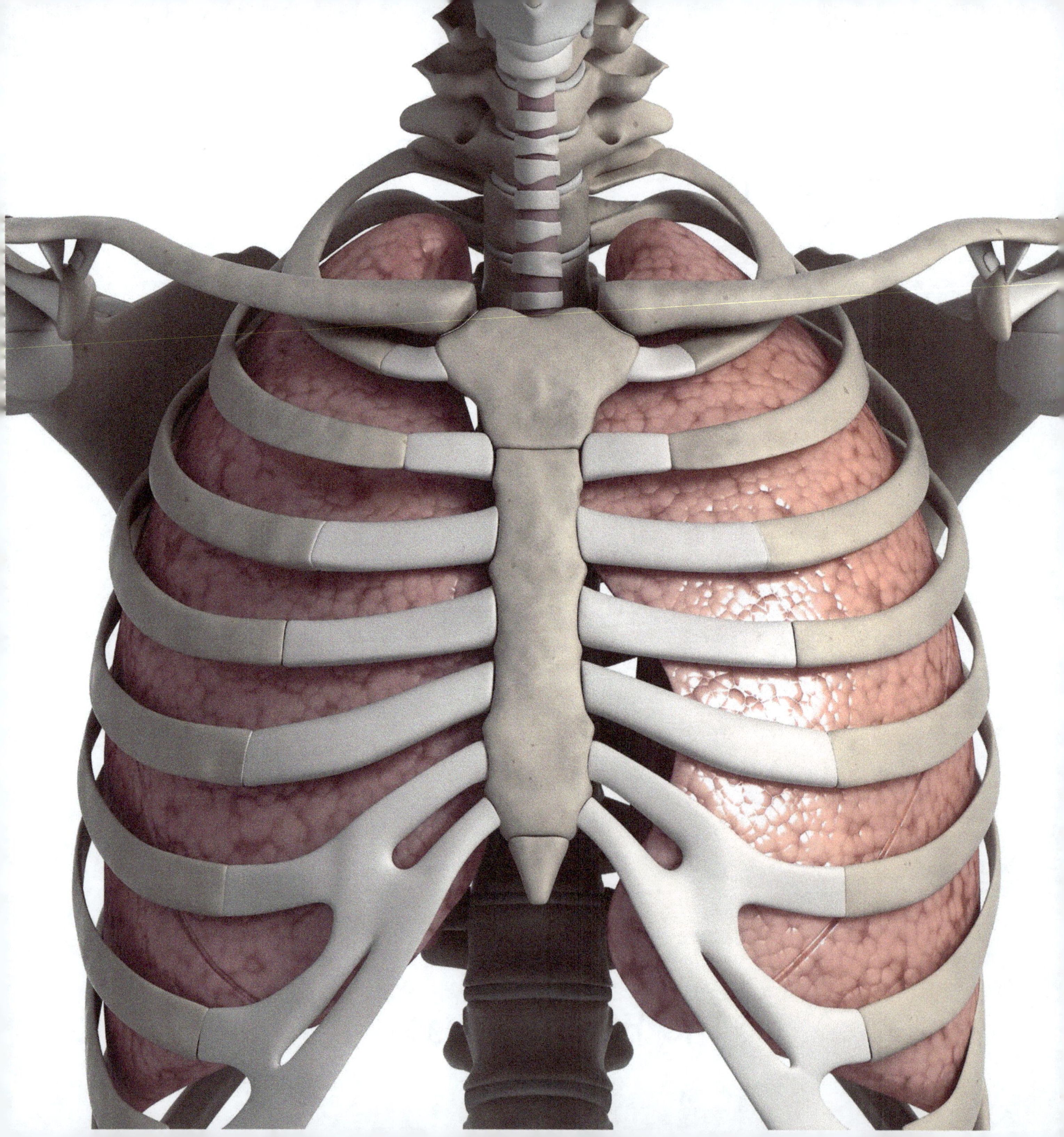

You also breathe out carbon dioxide, which your body doesn't need. There are hard bones inside your chest to protect your lungs from getting damaged. When you exercise and breathe deeply, it makes your lungs stronger. If you put a pair of human lungs in water, they would float. Your lungs are part of the respiratory system, which just means the system that helps you breathe.

THE PANCREAS

The pancreas is shaped something like a gun. It is located behind your stomach and is at the same level as your small intestine. When you eat, your pancreas lets out fluids. The fluids travel into a duct that goes into your small intestine. The fluids have a lot of enzymes. They help to break down the nutrients in the food you eat, like proteins, fats, and carbohydrates.

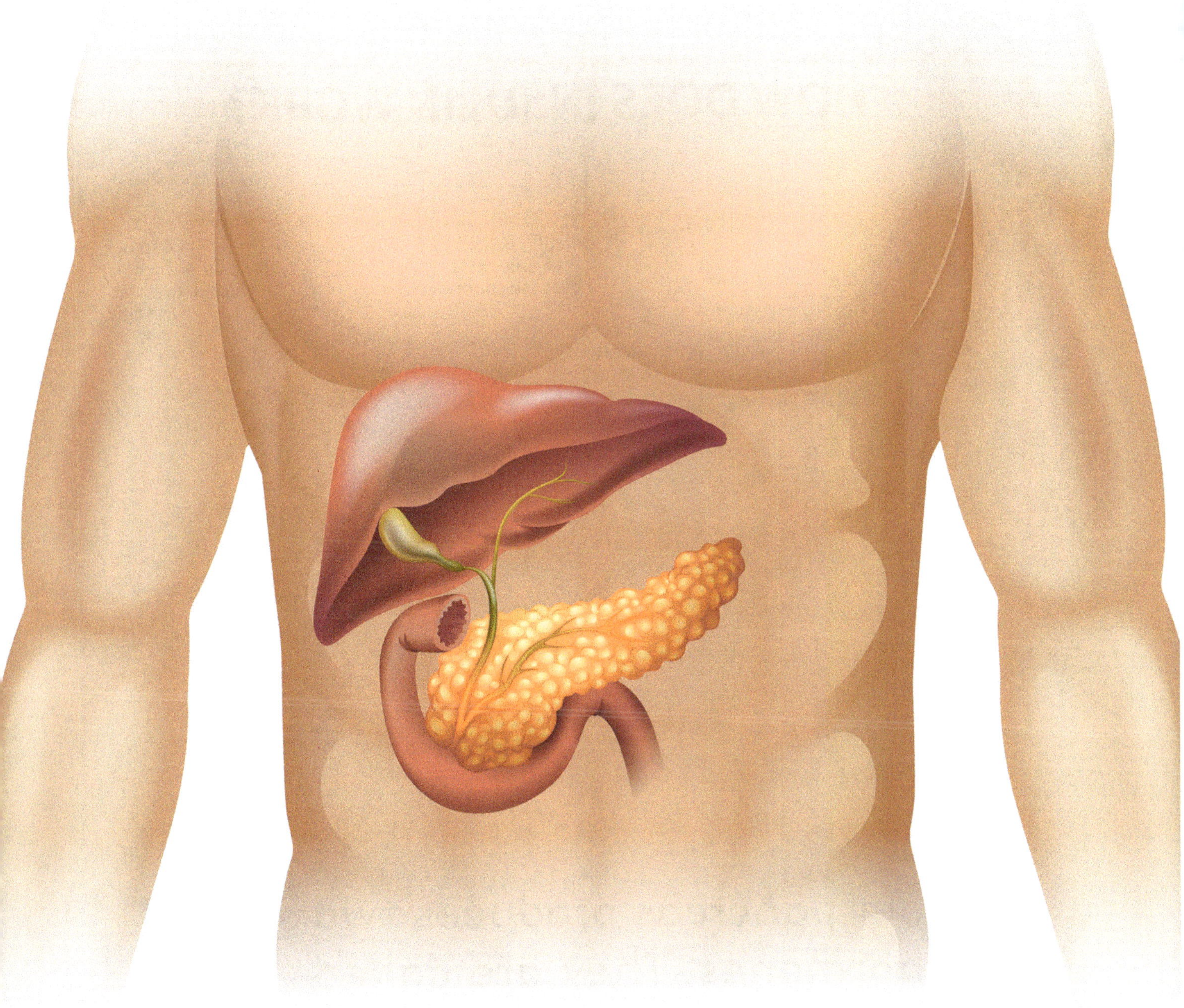

The Pancreas

HOW DOES INSULIN WORK?

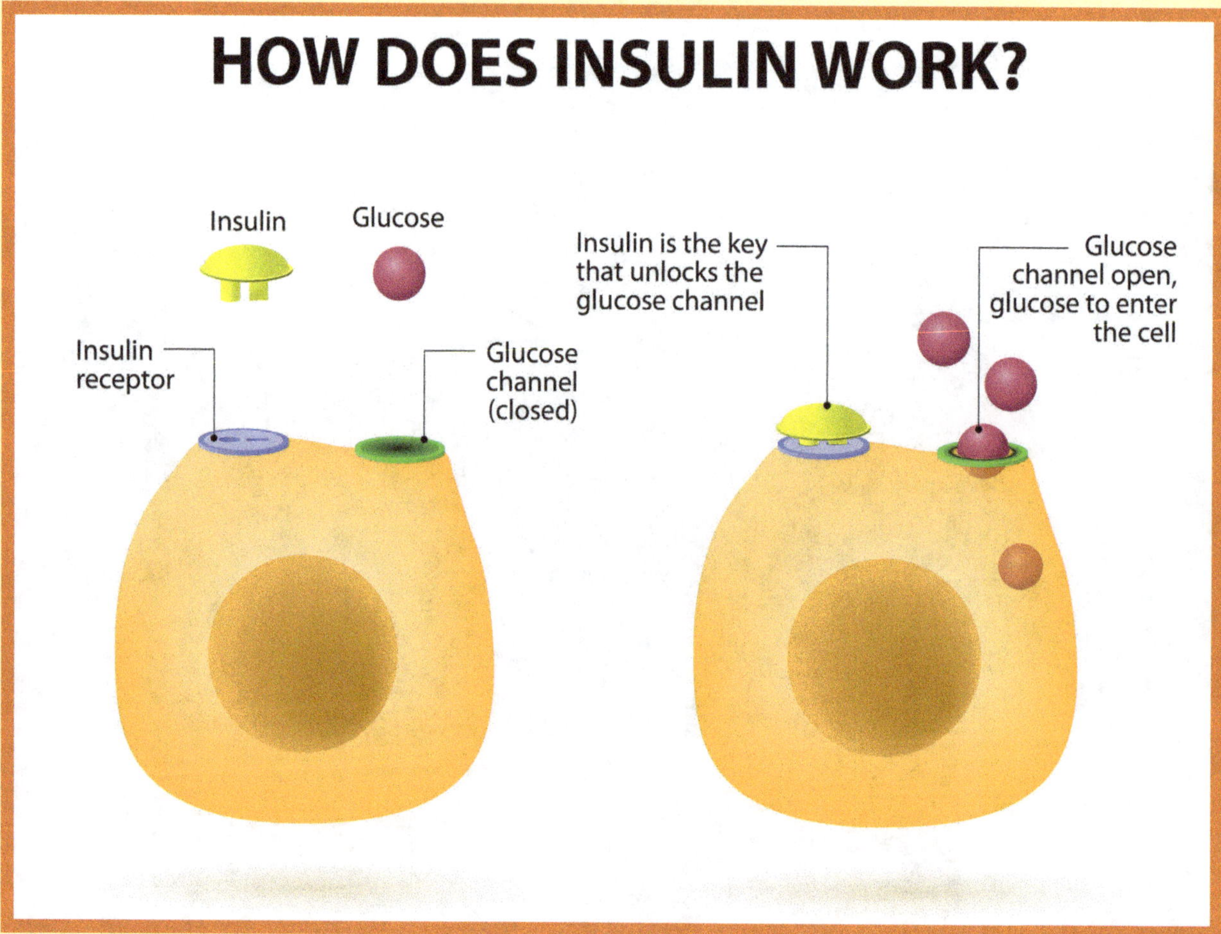

Your pancreas produces two special hormones. They are called insulin and glucagon.

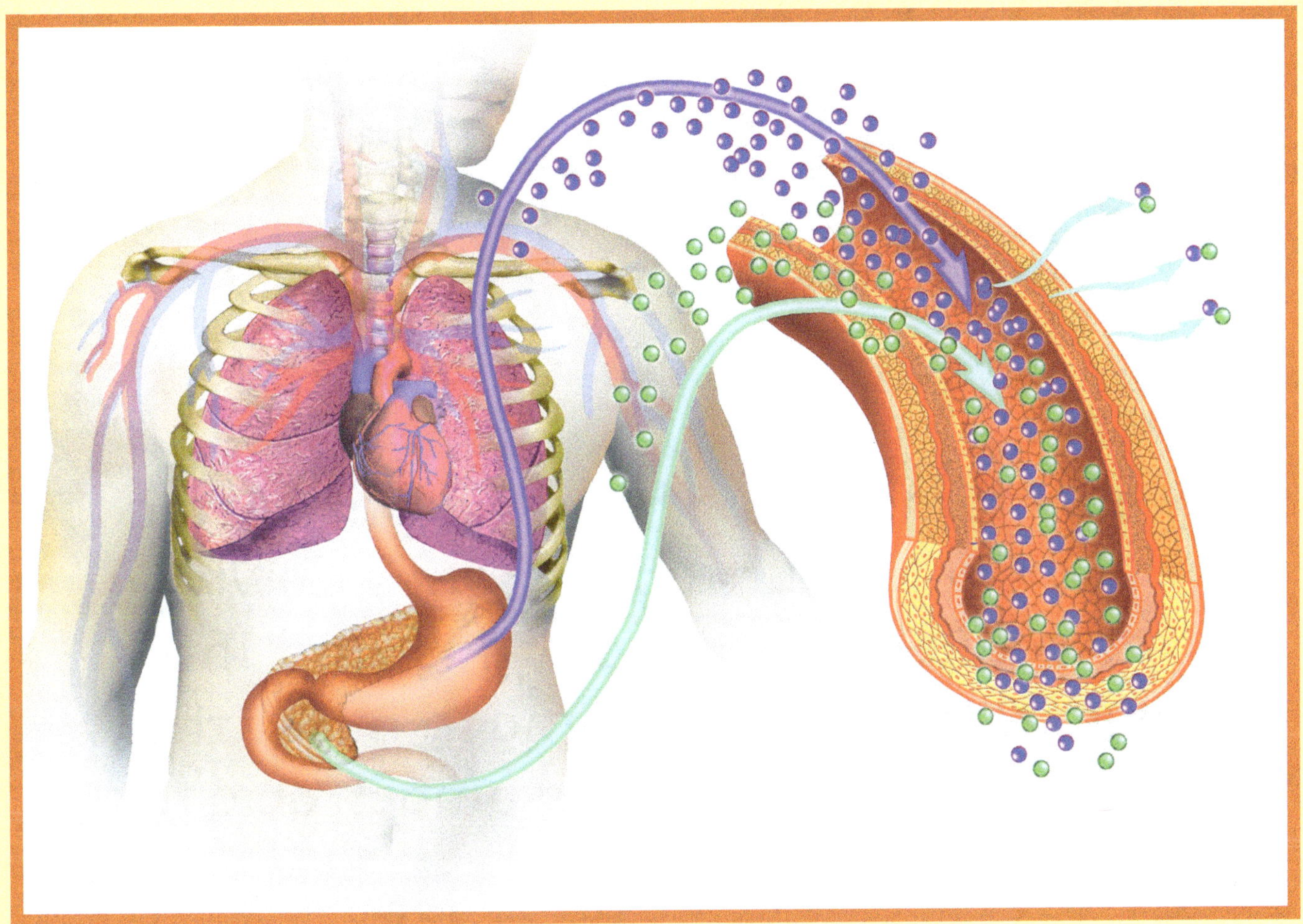

They help keep the level of sugar in your blood in balance. The pancreas is part of the digestive system.

THE STOMACH

Your stomach is a hollow organ. After you chew your food, it goes down a tube called the esophagus and into your stomach. Your stomach mixes the chewed food with some stomach acid to break it down.

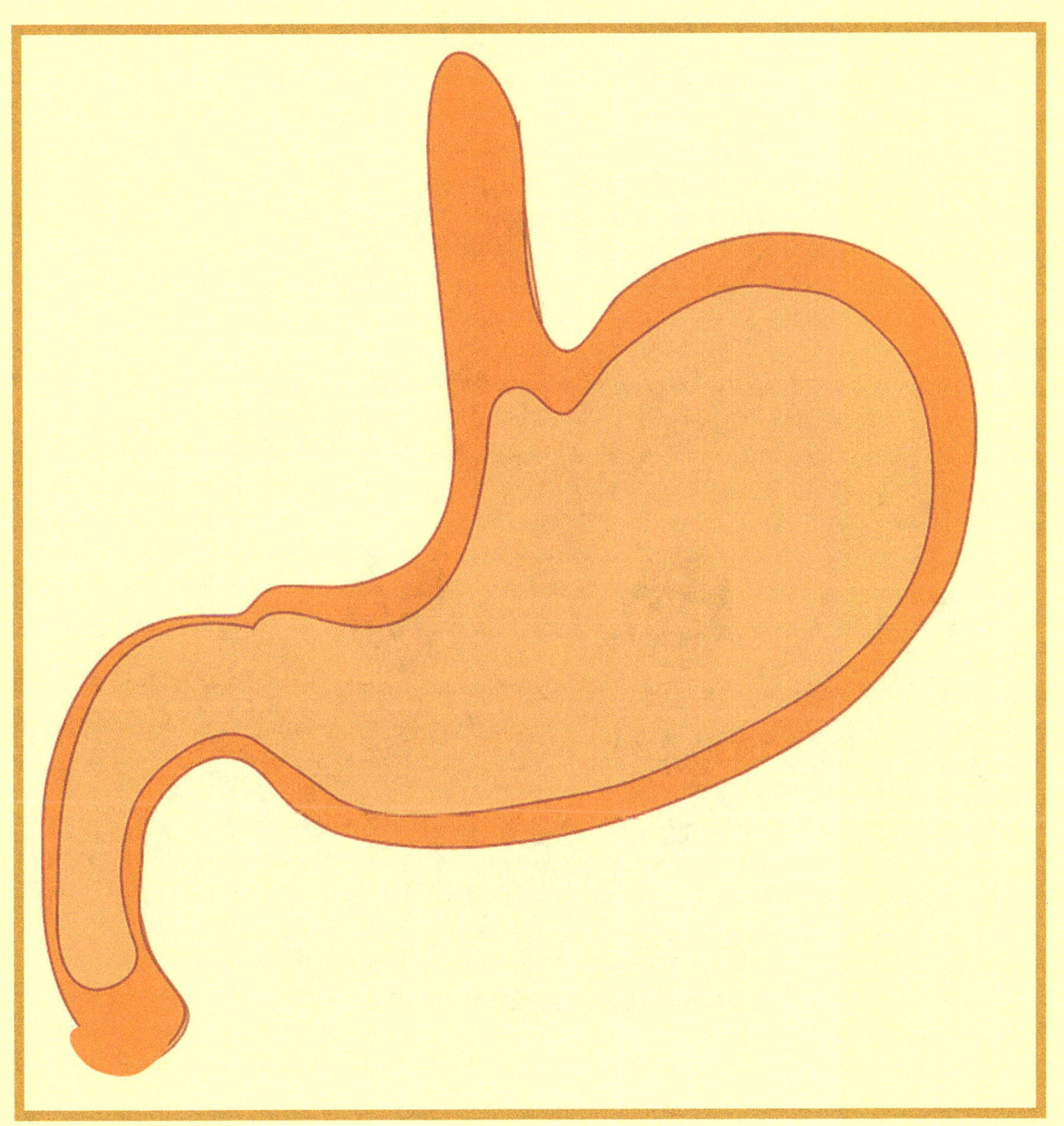

The Human Stomach

Oops! It's a Poop!

Once it's a liquid, your body can use the food for energy. Sometimes your stomach might get upset, if you eat something it doesn't like. Whatever your stomach doesn't use for energy, will eventually come out of your body as poop. Your stomach is part of your digestive system, which helps you process food.

THE SMALL INTESTINE

Your small intestine is connected to your stomach. It's the longest part of your digestive system. When you become an adult, your small intestine will be about 20 feet long. However, it isn't a straight line inside your body. Instead, it's all mashed up together like a bunch of hanging sausages.

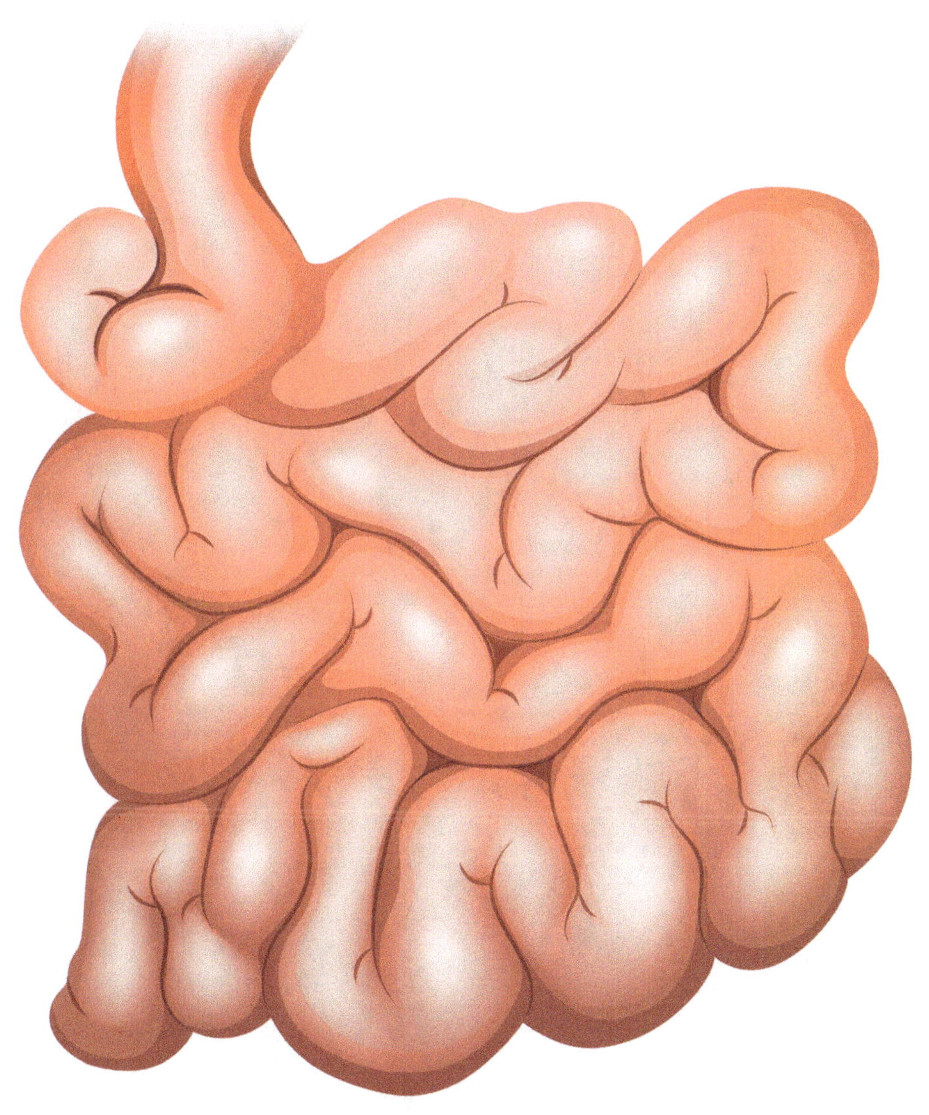

Small Intestine

Parts of the Abdomen

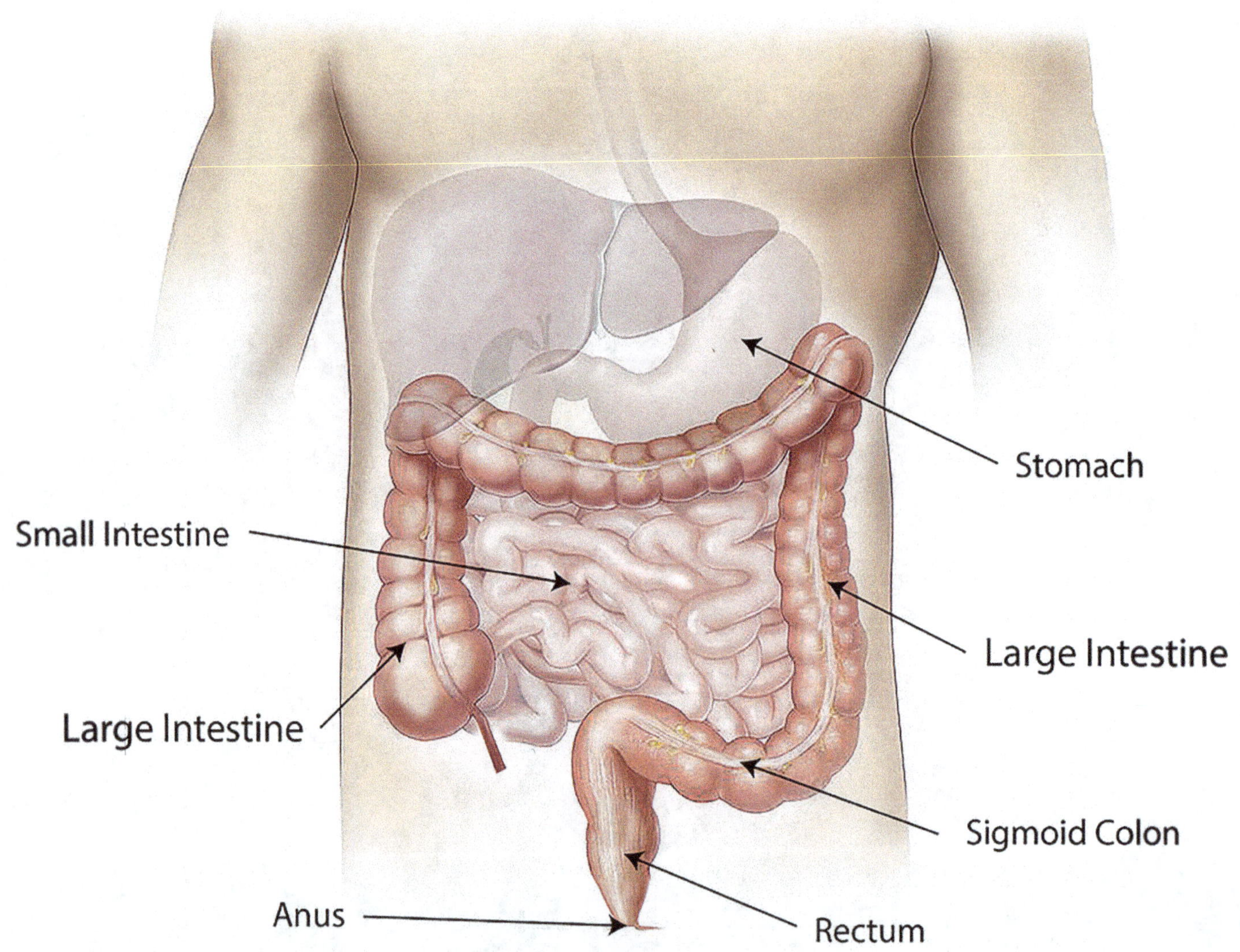

The small intestine is only about 1 inch in diameter. The job of the small intestine is to absorb the nutrients from the food that you eat. The inside of the small intestine has special tissues that feel like velvet. These tissues process the nutrients.

THE LARGE INTESTINE

Food that isn't digested goes into your large intestine from your small intestine. Your large intestine is about 3 inches in diameter. It is looped around your small intestine and attached to your rectum.

Anatomy of the Large Intestine

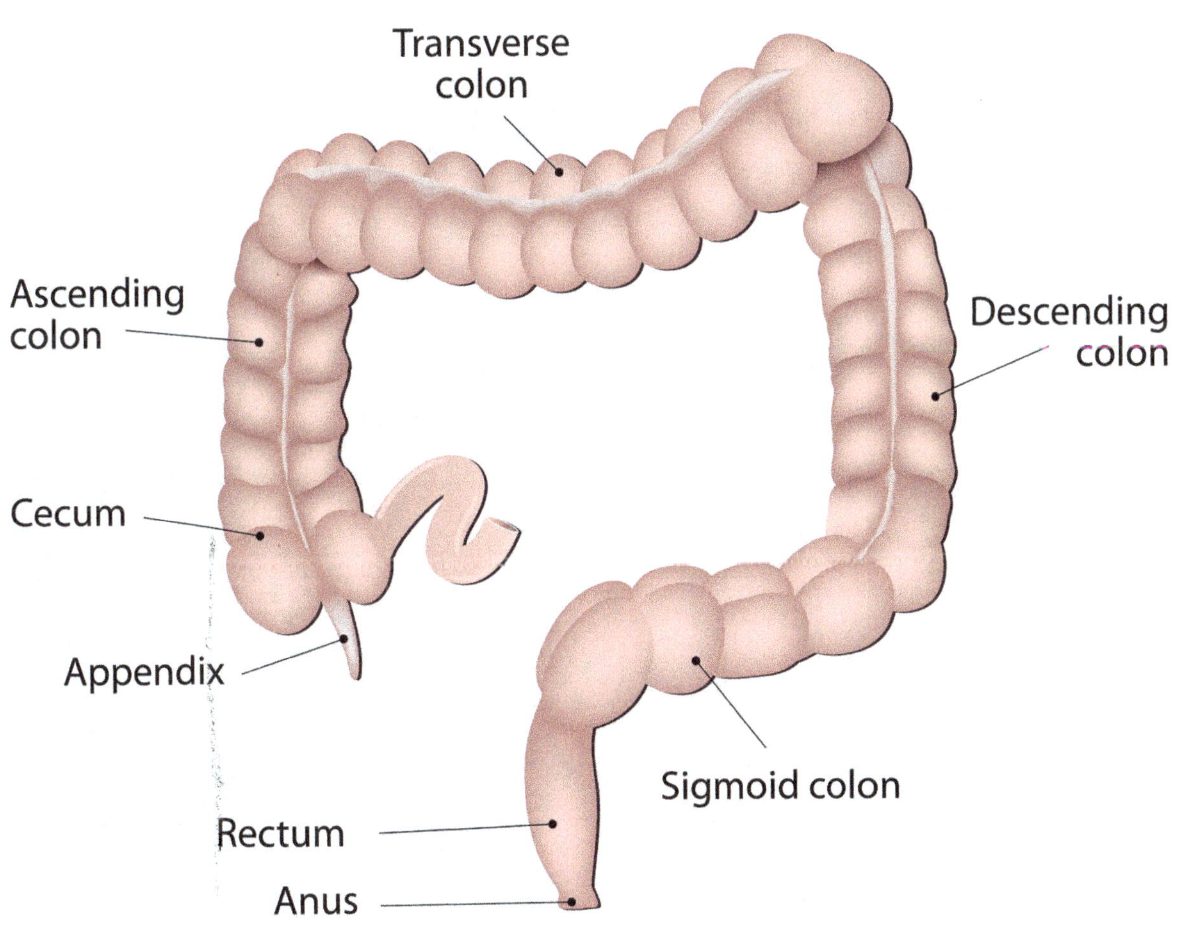

When you become an adult, your large intestine will be about 5 feet long. The main job of your large intestine is to take the leftovers from food and convert them to poop. The small intestine and the large intestine are part of the digestive system.

THE LIVER

You would die within a day if your liver stopped working. The liver is like a chemical factory. It's a spongy organ that is shaped like a wedge. Scientists believe that the liver does over 500 different jobs. It helps to get rid of substances like ammonia that are poisonous to your body. Like the pancreas, it helps to balance blood sugars.

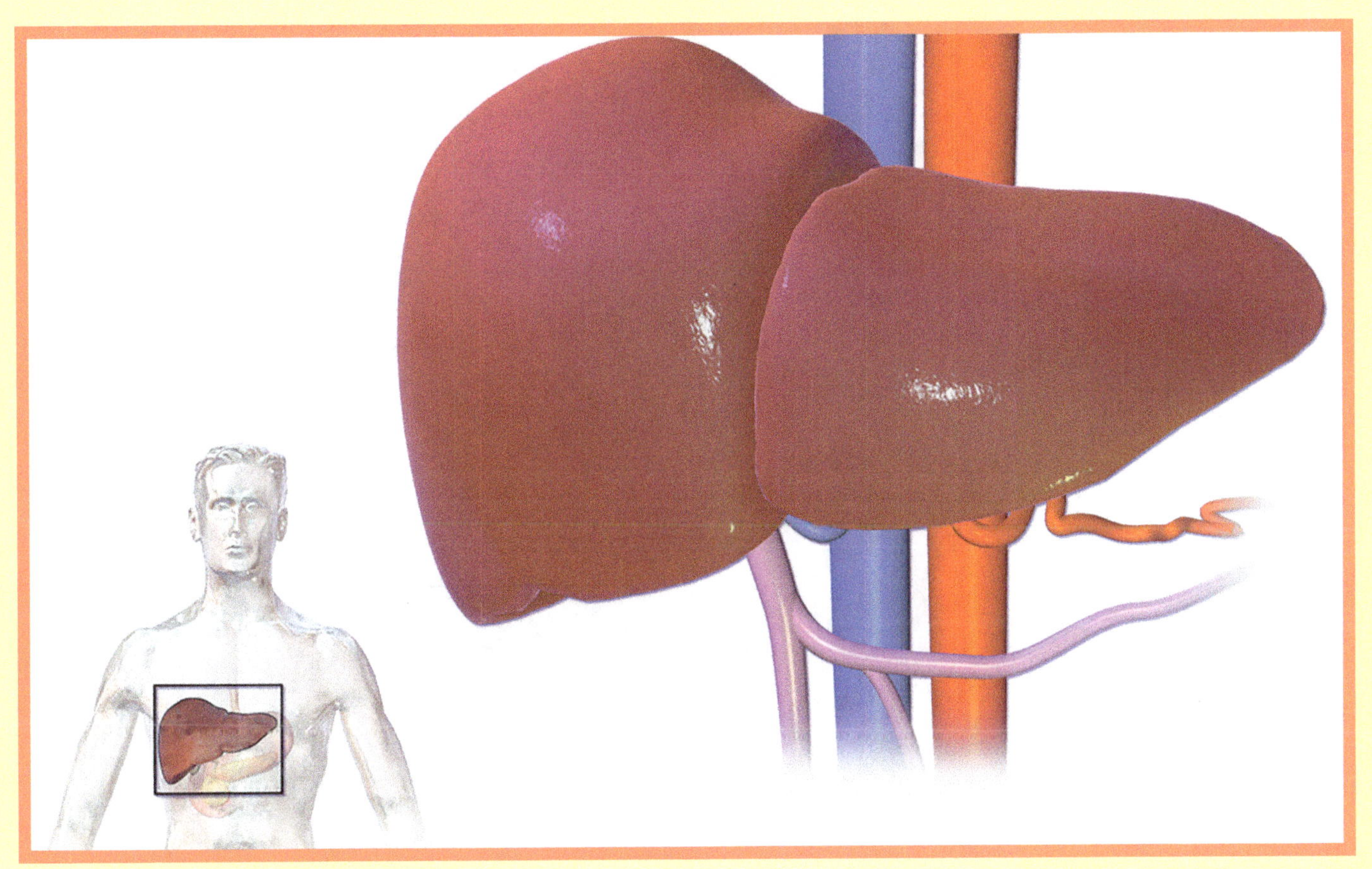

The Liver

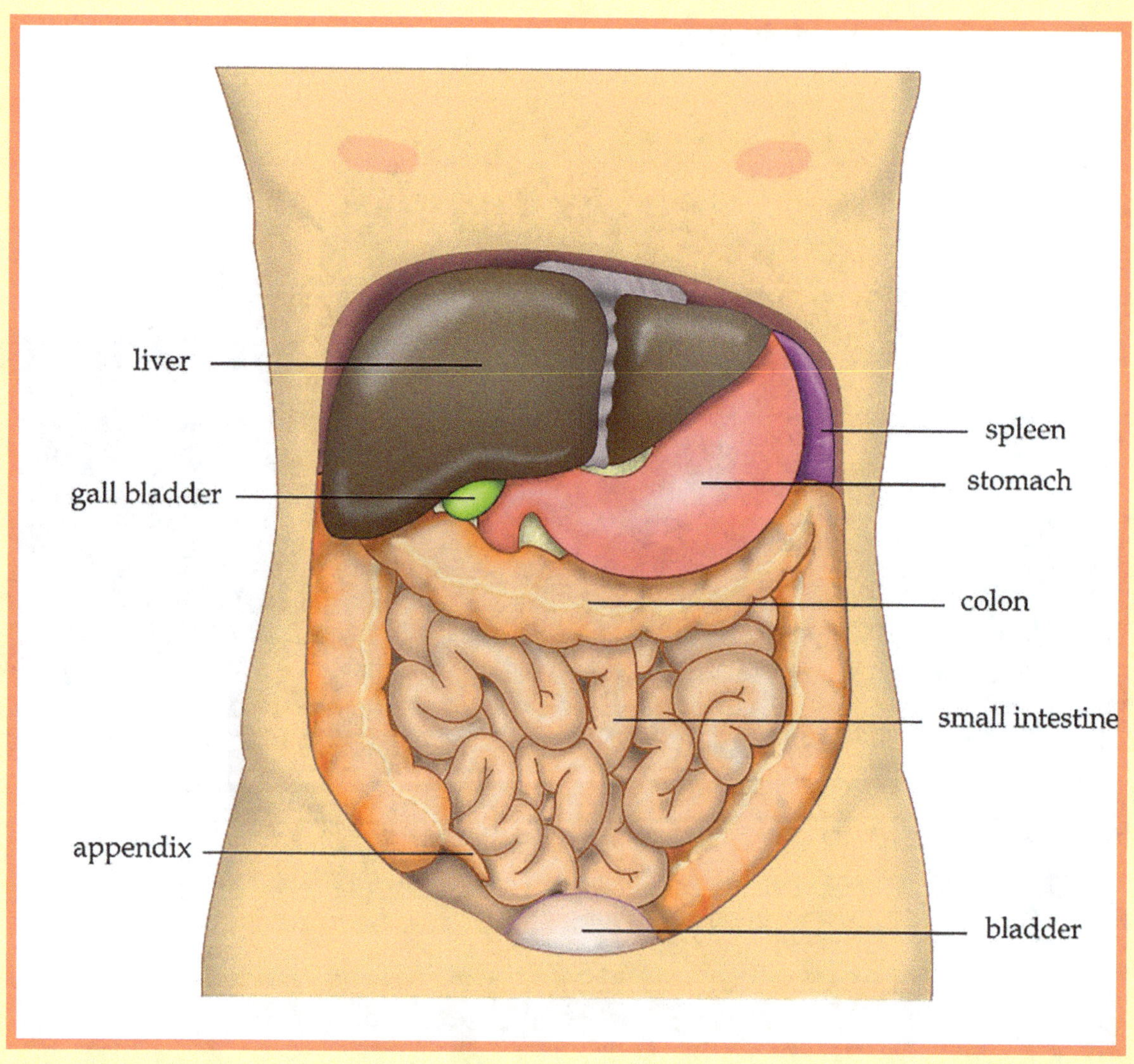

The liver is the largest internal
Organ of the human body.

The liver also changes the nutrients you eat in foods to forms that your cells can use. The liver is the largest organ inside your body and it is part of the digestive system. It produces bile, a green liquid that helps you digest fat.

THE KIDNEYS

You have two kidneys and they are each about the size of your fist. They are a blood-red color and they are shaped like the kidney beans you use to make chili. The function of the kidneys is to filter your blood continuously.

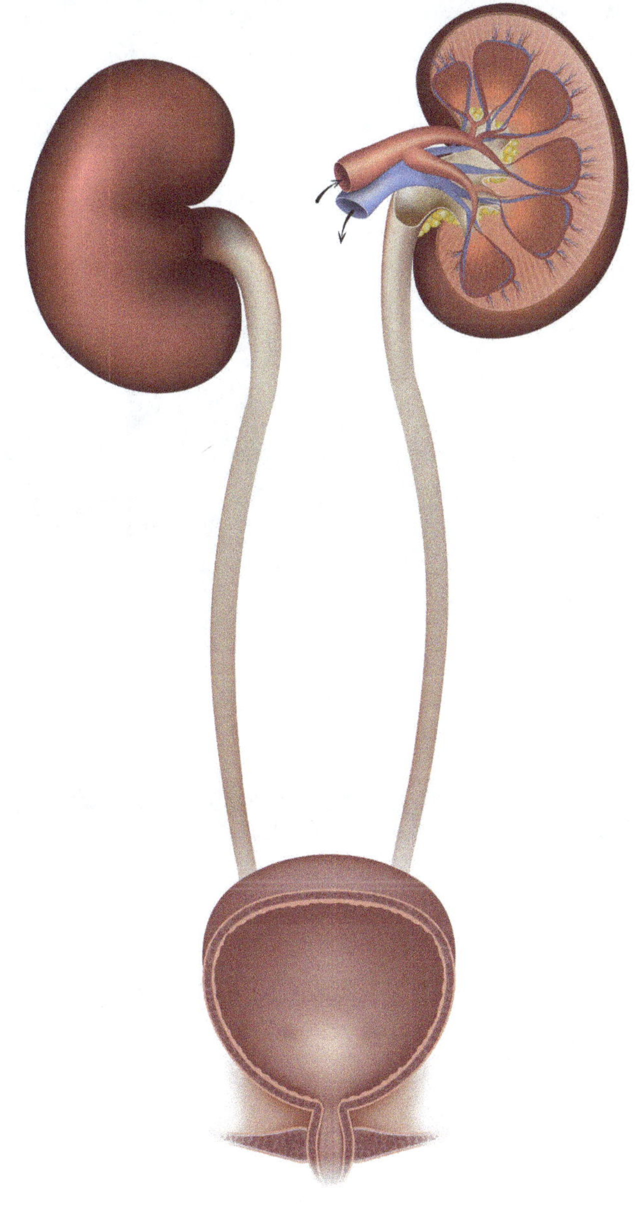

The Kidneys

They remove extra water and waste from your blood to make your pee, which is also called urine. Every minute, one fourth of the blood in your body goes through your kidneys. The kidneys filter things in and out of your blood to keep it in the best balance.

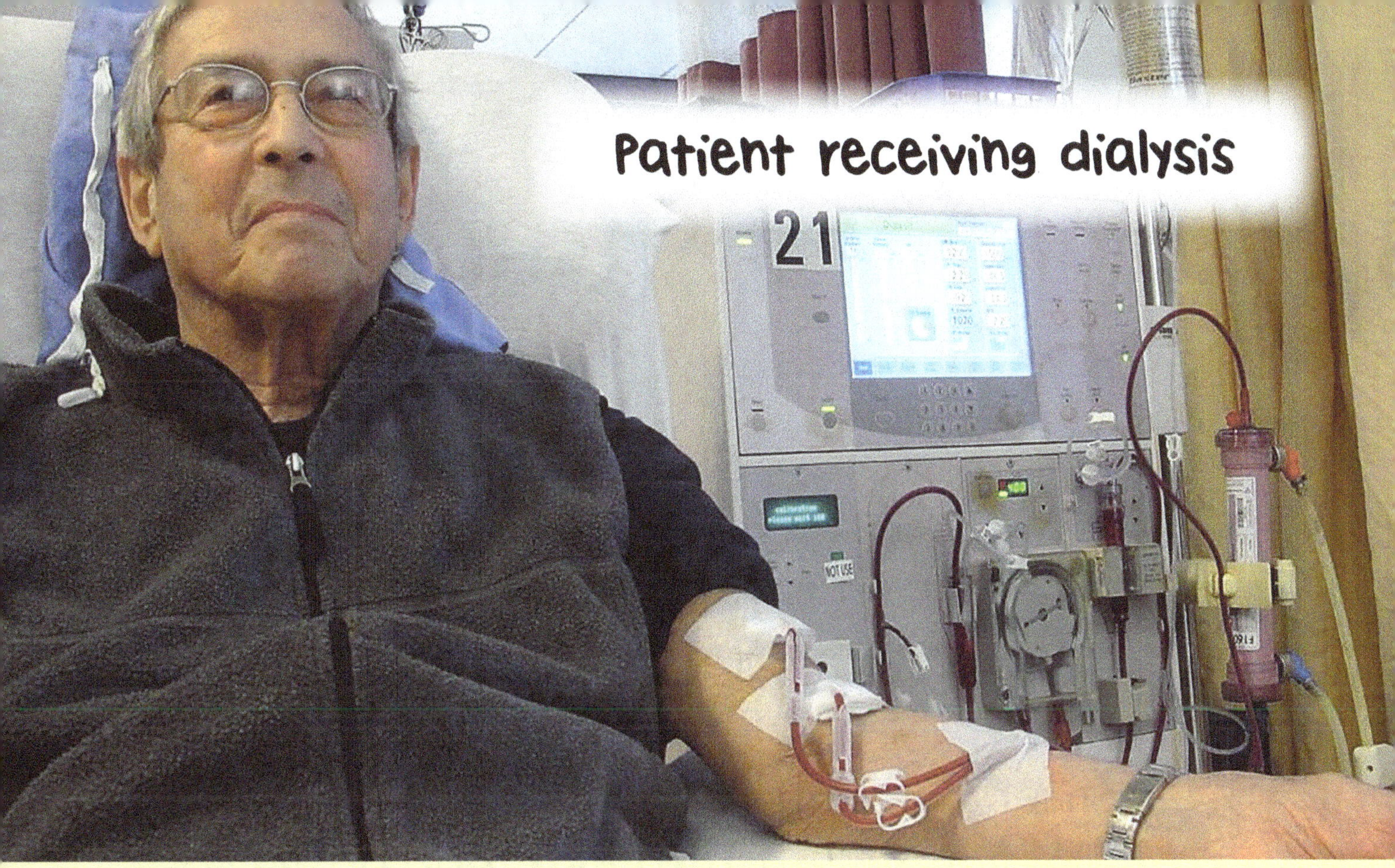

You can live with just one kidney. However, if most of the function of your kidneys is lost you have to use a dialysis machine. Some people who have kidney failure have kidney transplants. They get a kidney from someone else.

THE SPLEEN

Your spleen is part of your lymphatic system, which simply means that it helps you fight infection. Your spleen is a filter for cleaning your blood. It clears your blood of harmful bacteria as well as viruses. While your blood flows through, white blood cells go on the attack to remove any infection that could make you sick.

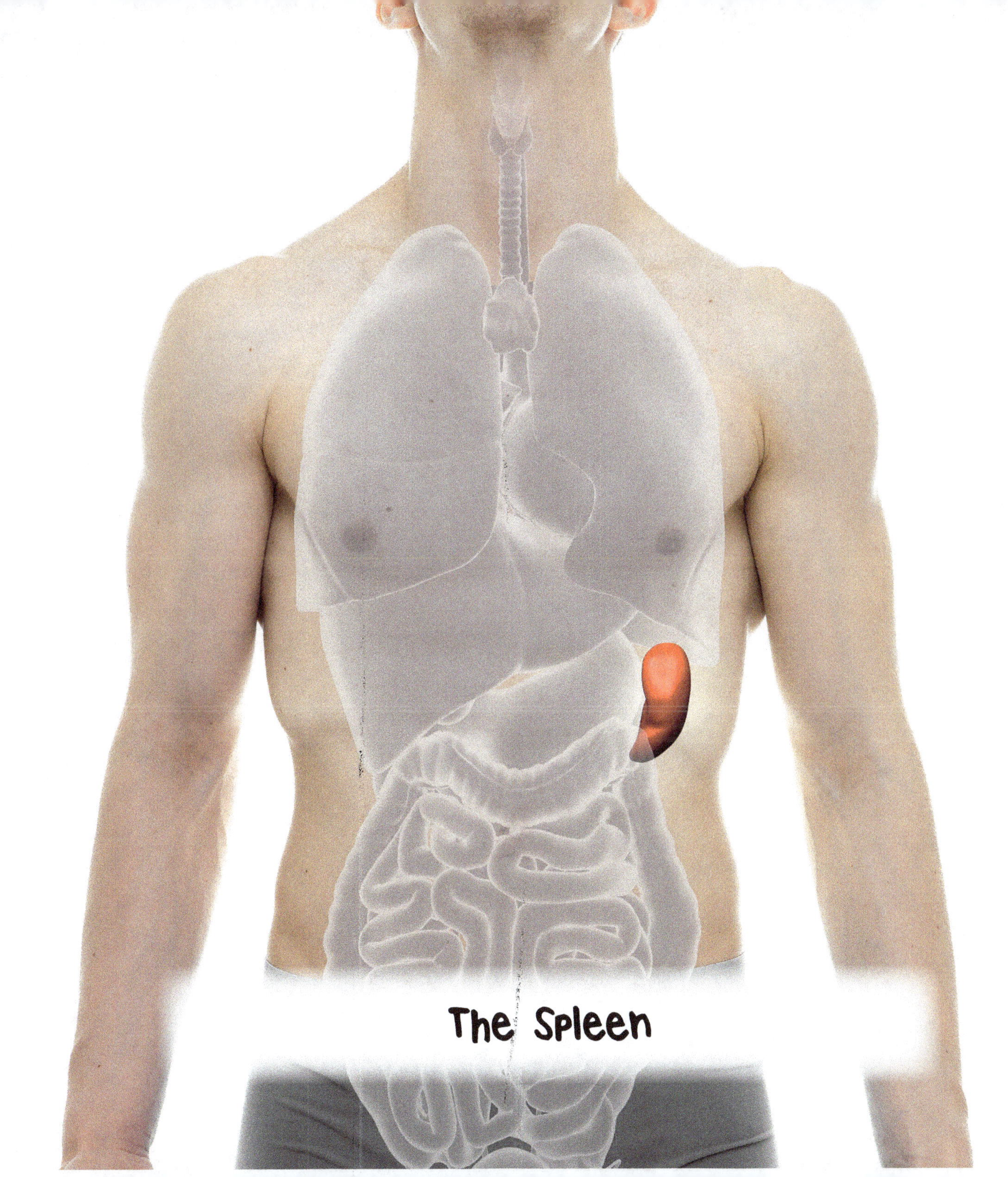

The Spleen

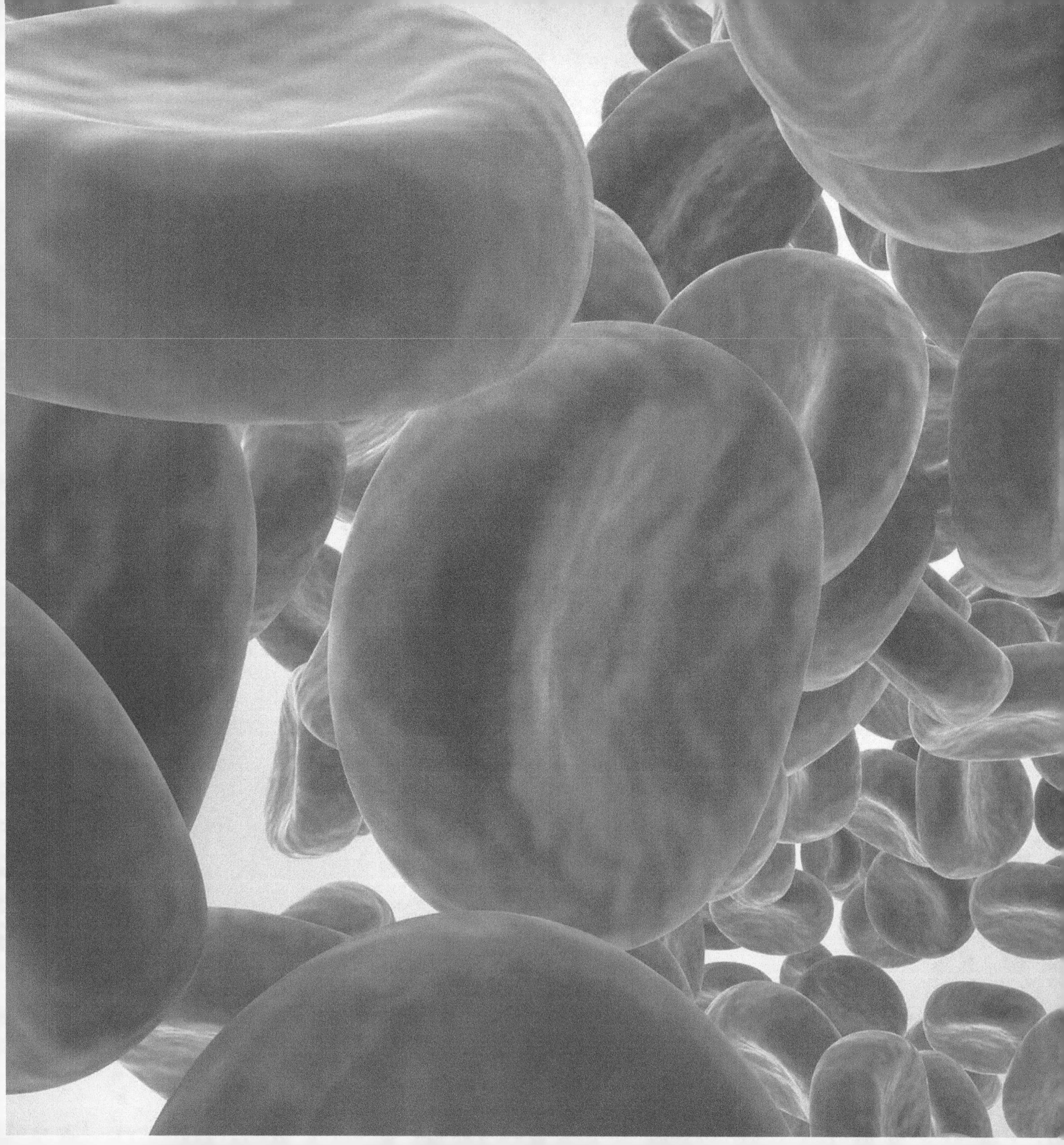

Your red blood cells only last about four months. Then, new ones must replace the old ones. Your spleen gets rid of the old red cells, while your bone marrow makes new ones. You can live without this organ and if something goes wrong with it, your other organs will take over most of its functions. However, you'll probably get more infections.

THE GALL BLADDER

The gall bladder is part of the digestive system. It's the storage container for the bile that your liver makes. It's a green sac that's shaped like a pear. After you eat, your gall bladder squeezes bile into your small intestine.

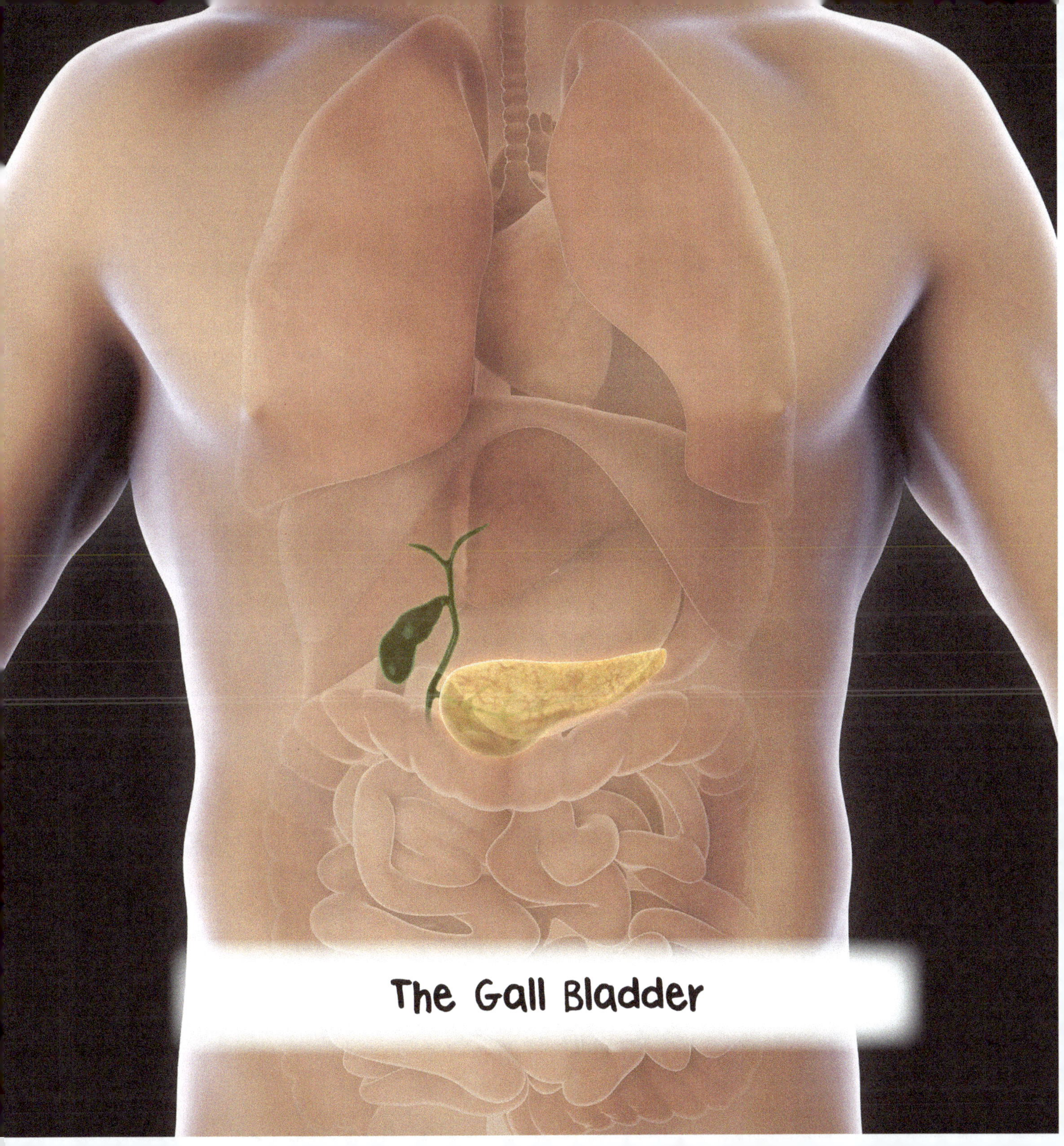

The Gall Bladder

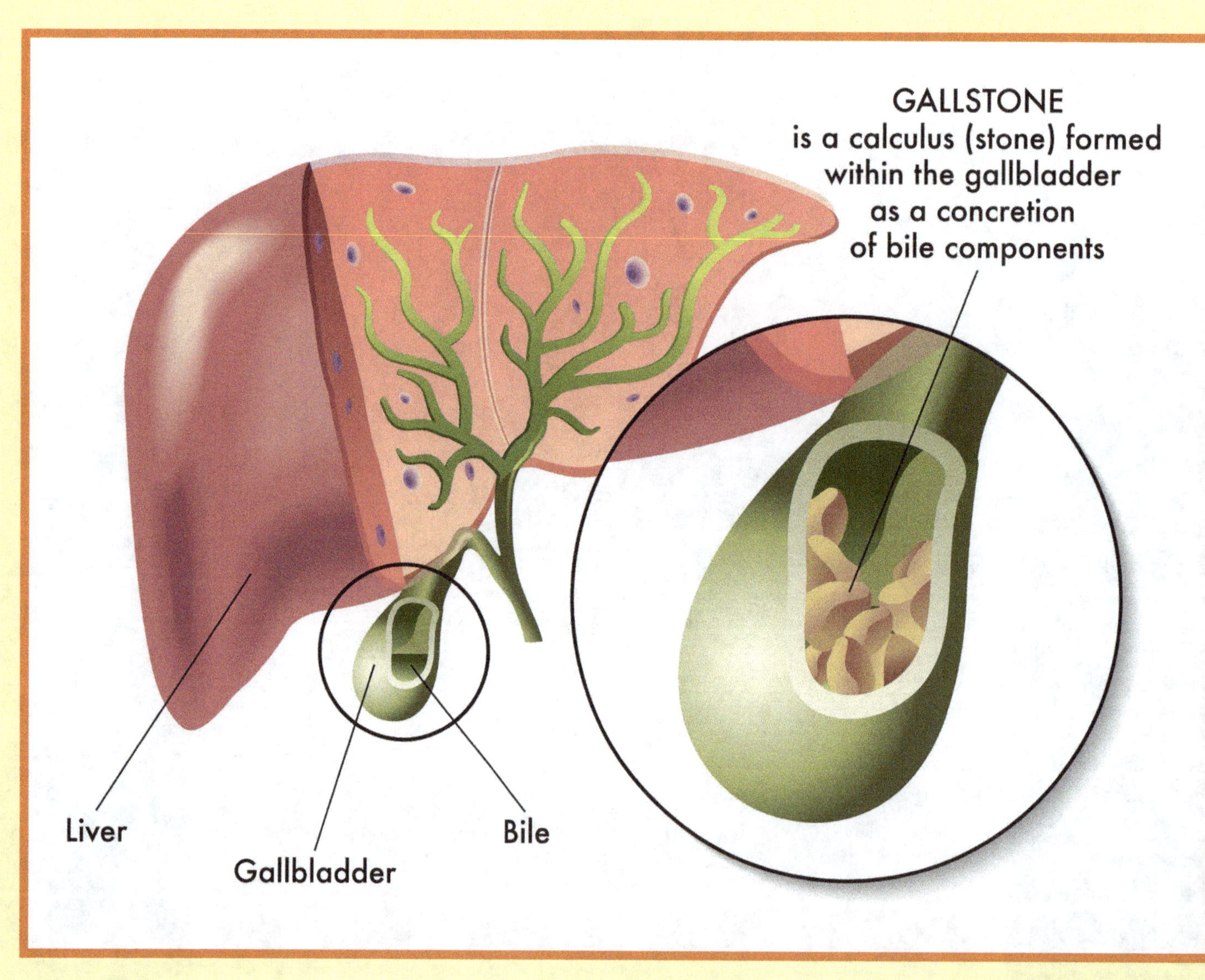

GALLSTONE
is a calculus (stone) formed
within the gallbladder
as a concretion
of bile components
Liver
Gallbladder
Bile

The purpose of the bile is to break down the fat that you eat. You produce about 1 liter of bile every day. Sometimes gall bladders form stones in them. If the stones get too large, they cause pain. You can live without a gall bladder.

THE SKIN

Your skin is the largest of the organs of your body and is part of a system with a long name, the integumentary system. Your skin, your hair, and your nails are all part of this system.

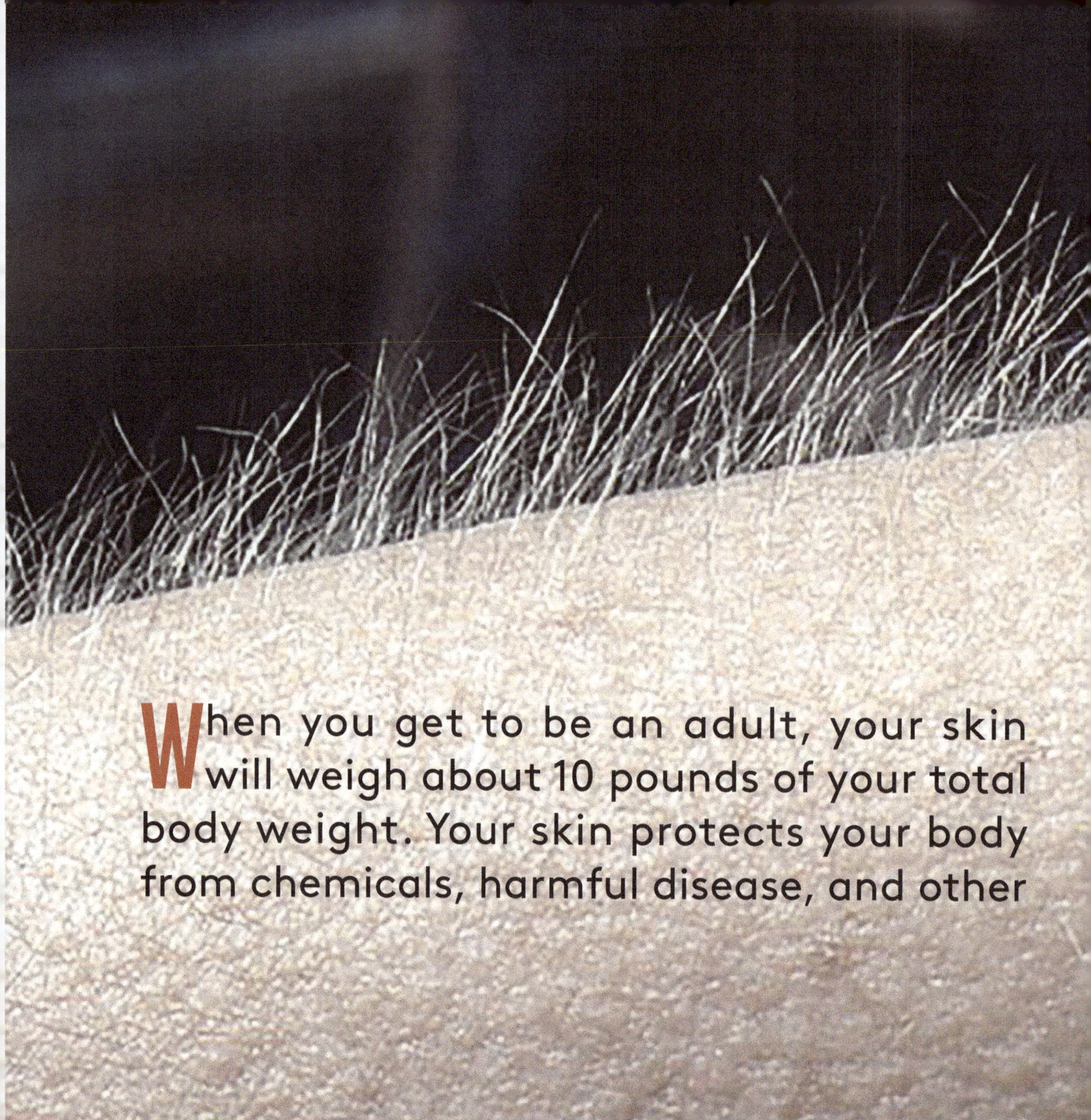

When you get to be an adult, your skin will weigh about 10 pounds of your total body weight. Your skin protects your body from chemicals, harmful disease, and other

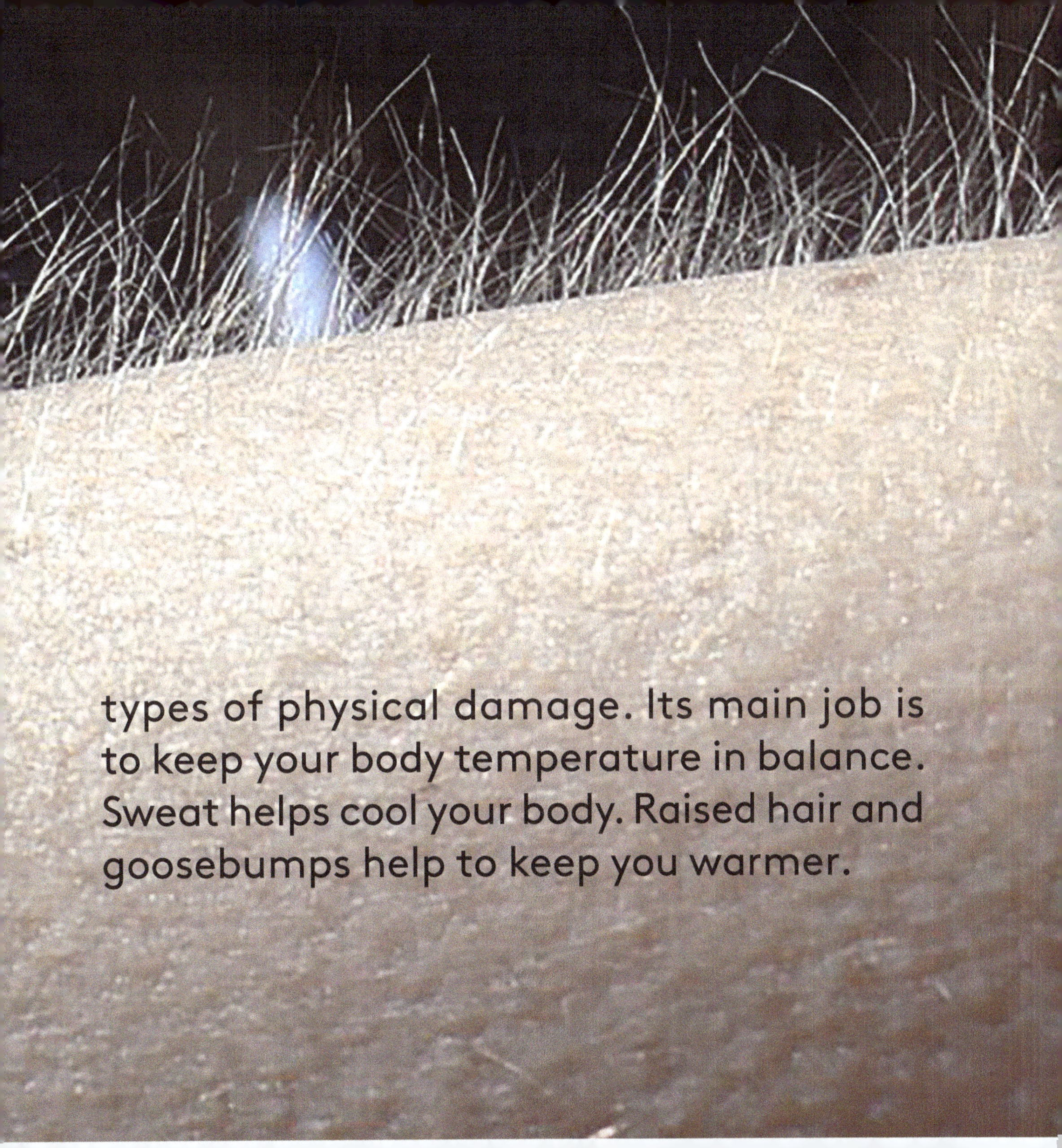

types of physical damage. Its main job is to keep your body temperature in balance. Sweat helps cool your body. Raised hair and goosebumps help to keep you warmer.

Awesome! Now you know more about the organs that make your body work. You can find more Biology books from Baby Professor by searching the website of your favorite book retailer.

Visit

BABY PROFESSOR
EDUCATION KIDS

www.BabyProfessorBooks.com
to download Free Baby Professor eBooks and view
our catalog of new and exciting Children's Books